Green Wate

An anthology cele
boats, vernacular I
lore; featuring the ... . Finlay,
Ian Stephen and Graham Rich.

Green Waters is published on the occasion of an
exhibition at The Pier Arts Centre, Stromness.

pocketbooks

A compendium of art forms and ideas,
Pocketbooks offer a generalist vision of
contemporary culture.

Pocketbooks are published collaboratively.
The Series is co-ordinated by Morning Star.

Series Editor	Alec Finlay
Assistant Editor	Gavin Jones
Associate Designer	RedLetter
Associate Publisher	Polygon

Editorial address	Morning Star
	P O Box 23143
	Edinburgh EH3 8YQ

U.K. Distributor	Scottish Book Source
	137 Dundee Street
	Edinburgh EH11 1BG

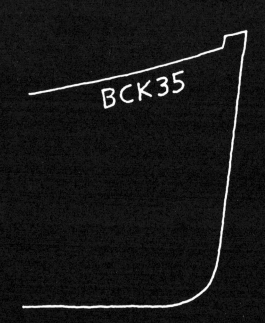

BCK35

PROEM

Green Waters

An Anthology of Boats & Voyages

Green Waters

featuring

IAN HAMILTON FINLAY
IAN STEPHEN
GRAHAM RICH

Edited by Alec Finlay

The Pier Arts Centre, Stromness
Polygon, Edinburgh
Morning Star, Edinburgh
Taigh Chearsabhagh, Lochmaddy

1998

Published by

The Pier Arts Centre, Stromness
Polygon, Edinburgh
Morning Star, Edinburgh
Taigh Chearsabhagh, Lochmaddy

Set in Sabon

Typography by RedLetter, Edinburgh
Typeset by Smith Settle, Otley
Designed by Morning Star and RedLetter
Printed and bound by Smith Settle

Published with the assistance of a grant
from the Scottish Arts Council

THE SCOTTISH **ARTS** COUNCIL

A CIP record is available from the British Library

ISBN 0 9527669 2 2

List of Contents

The bow soars, finds the waves
The hull accepts.
George Oppen

from Ian in LS to Pia in HH

from Ian in SY to Barbara in SY

from Graham in E to Lesley in E

from Eck in EH to Zoë in LO

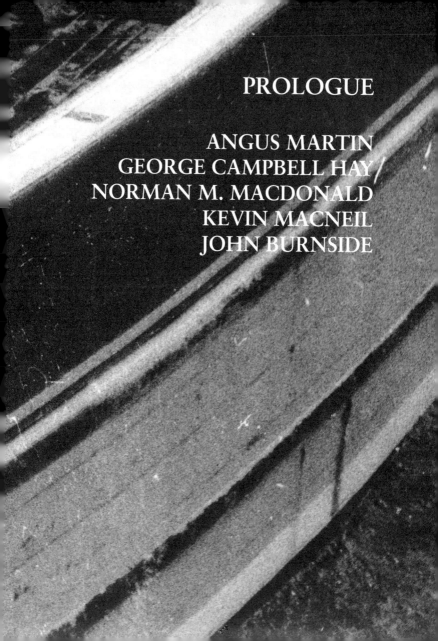

PROLOGUE

ANGUS MARTIN
GEORGE CAMPBELL HAY
NORMAN M. MACDONALD
KEVIN MACNEIL
JOHN BURNSIDE

Always Boats and Men

Always boats and men
crowding quiet vision
when I am alone
and thinking back.

Deserted harbours, ruins keeping
to themselves, the sea at evening
where fleets were crowded once,
faint chorusing of gulls.

I am seeking the one thing
to say that will say all
that is unsaid, that I may
be done with it; but there are only

images in memory
like sunlight on the sea
which is a wholeness but
broken millionfold within.

Angus Martin

from **Seeker Reaper**

She's a solan, she's a tramper, she's a sea-shaker,
she's a hawk, she's a hammer, she's a big-sea-breaker,
she's a falcon, she's a kestrel, she's a wide-night-seeker,
she's a river, she's a render, she's a foam-spray-waker.
She's a stieve sea-strider, she's a storm-course-keeper,
she's a tide-scour-bucker, she's a quick-light-leaper,
she's a stem-tearer, keel-tearer, seeker, finder, reaper.
She's *Cast off! Anchor up!* deid anchor-weary,
she's a chain-snubber, moorin'-strainer, restless herbour peerie.
She's a skyline-raiser, skyline-sinker, hulldown horizon-crosser,
She's foreland, foreland, on and on, a high-heid-tosser.
She's a glint, she's a glimmer, she's a glimpse, she's a fleeter,
she's an overhauler, leave-astern, a hale-fleet-beater;
she's a kyle-coulter, knot-reeler, thrang-speed-spinner,
her mood is moulded on her and the mind that made her's in her.
She's a wake-plough, foam-plough, spray-hammer, roarer,
she's a wind-anvil, crest-batterer, deep-trough-soarer,
she's a dance-step-turner, she's a broad-wake-scorer,
She's a sound-threider, bight-stringer, her hert runs oot afore her.
When the big long seas come on lik walls, cold-white-heided,
she doesna flinch a point for them. Straight her wake is threided.

George Campbell Hay

Zulu-Fishing

Always you stare at the purple water, looking for the smoking signs of the herring. It's good when the water's dark for then you can imagine it swimming with fish.

When the water's clear you're sailing over safe sandy bottom, nothing to be seen but the green smooth ground. A crab slides along sideways. A speckled plaice stirs up the sand like a puff of smoke. Gone at once like blood in the water. Yes we like the deep indigo sea. Even though the colour also hides the rocks, it hides the fish from us, we say, planting the nets.

We say to each other, "They're down there in shoals, millions. Soon they'll be in our nets, a years money in one night!"

After the psalm and the supper and the waiting, the hauling of the nets, the capstan turning, we shake out the gasping fish, the hold fills, the boy coils, coils in his wet cubbyhole, in his heaving world of black wet rope.

We turn for home. Portrona beckons in the pearl and gold dawn. The wind with us, she takes it, hear her hiss through the water. The Zulu boat heeling, straining boards and sheets and canvas. Hear her chuckle past Tiumpan, Bayble-Island, the Chicken. She heels so far, at the Beasts, herring slips from her decks back into the sea.

Arnish, Goat Island, Number One. Portrona Quay before us. We're not the first but we're not the last either.

Norman Malcolm MacDonald.

Joy in the Hebrides

One day, they pushed the boat out. He rowed unspeakingly and in a few lengthening minutes they were a considerable distance from the shore. It was looking, as they say in Stornoway, very *mì-chàilear*. The sky was a marbled print, porridgy grey and watery blue. The great bulk of seawater slapped its unthinking rhythm on the creaking body of the boat. He pulled the sleeves of his *geansaidh* down over his clammy hands.

Her face opposite him shone with its usual lunar paleness. It occurred to him that she was scrutinising his own face as though searching for something new. He paused, then moved over to her. He leaned in close, observing that, like a Celtic manuscript, all her beauty was in the detail. The dolphinsmooth curves of her cheekbones, the dawnstained miniature pillows of her lips, the ovenbread mist of her flesh.

When their lips touched, they seemed to bring about a small electric charge. Her warm tongue slithered into his mouth, all strawberries and milk.

When he withdrew, when he opened his eyes, the light around them seemed to have strengthened, as though everything were reflected in highly polished silver.

At that moment, though, without warning, he felt a third presence nibbling like a squirrel at the edge of his joy. His father's boat was rounding the Rubha Glas like a gangster, like an ex-boyfriend.

He blinked suddenly, smacked the oars down and spun the boat round.

Kevin MacNeil

Fisherfolk at Newhaven

after Hill and Adamson

Mending their nets
                     or standing in their dim
smoke houses
               hearing the water
slap against the wood-face of the dock

and thinking of nights at sea
                         of a spilt
quiver of brindled fish
on the slur of the deck

of calling back and forth through lanternlight
for uncles and second cousins
to come and look:

the fruits of the ocean
                         tarred with a difficult blue
as they haul them in
siren faces poised
                 as if to speak

but silent
            like the wives they leave behind
for weeks and months
                            beguiled by the wounded skins
they bring in from the dark
                            the slatted crates

dripping with salt and copper
                            and the pale
shimmer of phosphorescence
                            like the chill
that grows between their hands
                            on chapel days.

John Burnside

GREEN WATERS

IAN HAMILTON FINLAY
IAN STEPHEN

Green Waters

Green Waters
Blue Spray
Grayfish

Anna T
Karen B
Netta Croan

Constant Star
Daystar
Starwood

Starlit Waters
Moonlit Waters
Drift

Ian Hamilton Finlay

Providence

Kippers on your breath and
the washed smell of your hair.

Providence, Strathgarry, Fiery Cross.
The Arnish light and the beacon.

Courteous signals in your tones:
your green and disarming eyes.

Golden Sheaf, Comrade, Northern Star.
A fixed navigational sequence

below the night cloud line
and October star-points.

Tension of wind-drift and keel
in the tracings of wakes.

Ian Stephen

Vernacular Shaping of a Sailing Hull

To make way through water,
carrying a given load,
wetness is replaced by air
to a width and depth
judged necessary
without risk to the strength
of the total structure.

A buoyant body and
the salient part – a fin.
They conjoin in a radius
so a flat plate on edge
meets upper lift.
The two are united by
the method of construction:
a half eggshell and
the rearranged plate.

When going faster,
wave-making friction
becomes important.
A half-ball has
the maximum displacement
for the surface shown
but the boat below the body
becomes narrow.

The full hull is a
pure shape, distorted –
cheeks sucked-in
by experience.

The more you stretch
the hull outwards,
the keel down,
the more wetted surface
you've got.

Resistance is not all bad.
A big beam carries
a greater load and lends
force against heeling.
Keel resists drift.

Shape sheds a vortex
from off your stern-post.

A rotating barrel of water
left as your wake,
a line of ripples
just on one side
as the sail leans
to one side only.

The vessel negotiates
moving water:
its sails negotiate
moving air.

Leeway isn't
a measure of
imperfection.
The boat must make it
unless you're heading
dead downwind.

The angle of your heading
and the not-getting-there:
that difference
is leeway.
So when you're steering,
don't blame the boat.
You've to aspire to
more than your heading.

Remember that
boats are containers
to keep something in,
another thing out.
A waterproof vessel
has to contain
an absence of water.

If the inside and outside
are exchanged,
you're sunk.

Dissection proves
a boat is a structured shell
and not the solid body
you thought it was.

One half, lengthways,
is necessary and sufficient
to state the shape
of a specific hull.
One side devoid
of frames and boatskin
– a face fallen –
disturbs and reveals
behind varnished integrity.

Ian Stephen
Arranged from the words of Topher Dawson, boatbuilder

The English Colonel Explains an Orkney Boat*

The boat swims full of air.
You see, it has a point at both
Ends, sir, somewhat
As lemons. I'm explaining

The hollowness is amazing. That's
The way a boat
Floats.

Ian Hamilton Finlay

*from *Orkney Lyrics*.

River Exe

for Graham and Lesley

Back-eddy to Black Oar.
A nod to the Vicar of
Bridgwater's *Memory*.
Turf reach to Ting Tong pole.

Putting the tack in.

Upriver, upcurrent,
a diesel-assisted beat.
Returning by leaving
*Marks to Starboard.**

Ian Stephen

*by Robin Steavenson – a classic book on dinghy-racing.

Voyage In Sgoth *An Sulaire*

freed from clinging mist,
new rocks, cliffs, rough from the saw
that's it, our waypoint

diluted moon-pull
leads our vessel's nosing prow
through calcified fins

the rounding tumble
over seabird stereo screech
we've come too close

outlying skerries sprawl
disrupting a lifetime's fetch
these broken waters

our bow's a chisel
we leave wet seriphs astern
a hissing exhale

spurdog swell turns back
from the bay's tight confinement
– a grey rasping tail

three reefs help us in
to the anchor on the chart
fisherman bites kelp

Ian Stephen

Proverbs

(1)   Cross-
         winds
         straight
         wakes

(2)   Black-
         water
         Brightling-
         sea

(3)   Bilges
         beget
         rainbows

(4)   Keels
         before
         colours

(5)   A feather
         takes
         the helm

Ian Hamilton Finlay

Fiddle-Tune Titles

for Alasdair Fraser

Hornpipe
The Driftwood Skip at Zero Longitude.

March
The Vicar of Whatsitsnames's good ship *Memory*.

Strathspey
Broad Bay's Return To Loch Eriboll.

Jig
The Buddhist Buoys of Pittenweem.

Ian Stephen

**Five Poems for Nine Planks:
the Shape of Westray Skiff *Emily***

slow the tree and let the timber ring

sap-damp planking needs a breathing flow

clinker lines behind the dusty spray

boatskin supple straight from the steamer

copper clenching lets the membrane stretch

Ian Stephen

Hesiod:
An Epigram on the Common Fisheries Policy

All that we did not want to catch, we kept, and all that
we wanted to take home we throw over the side.

XVII in *The Epigrams of Homer*

The original (according to Loeb) reads: "All that we caught
we left behind, and all that we did not catch we carry home"
– seemingly a reference to lice.

Ian Hamilton Finlay

creels and creels

creels and creels
creels and net-ropes
creels and men
net-ropes and net-ropes
men and creels and net-ropes
men and men

cobles and cobles
cobles and men and net-ropes
cobles and net-ropes
men and cobles
men and men

creels and cobles
creels and men and cobles
men and men

men and men

Eugen Gomringer, *cars and cars*.
Theocritus, *Idyll XXI*.

Ian Hamilton Finlay

After Theocritus – *Idyll XXI*, lines 6-13

In a ramshackle hut just above the tidemark
two old fishermen slept, their bed
some wizened seaweed, and beside them
an old patched coble, creels and lines.
Such a poor dwelling. And their blanket
a gansey stitched (it seemed) from net.

Ian Hamilton Finlay

The Inscriptions (for Carl Rakosi)

for Anthilla

               and for Archedike

Hediste and

             Hegesilla

Kallipe,

         Kleophonis,

                Melo

     (written   sgrafitto)

Mnesilla

      Rhodopis

and Sime

   who are

          beautiful

                &

          forgotten

Harry Gilonis

The Inscriptions (for Harry Gilonis)

for ~~Anthilla~~ Esther

and for ~~Archedike~~ Edith May

~~Hediste~~ Sara and

~~Hegesilla~~ Violet Sybil

~~Kallipe,~~ Clara

~~Kleophonis,~~ Veronica

~~Melo~~ Lily

(~~written~~ dark green and primrose ~~sgrafitto~~)

~~Mnesilla~~ Miranda

~~Rhodopis~~ Olive May

and ~~Sime~~ Ena

~~who are~~ whose lines

~~beautiful~~ were comely

&

~~forgotten~~ were taken

Ian Hamilton Finlay

37

Expectation*

The parents were asleep, the tall old clock ticked
monotonously, the wind sounded in the cracks in
the window frames while the moon's light from
time to time fell into the room. The young man lay
awake, feverishly thinking of the stories the stranger
had told. It is not material treasures which I desire,
he thought. But I do greatly desire to see the blue
sailboat. I cannot stop thinking about it, it haunts
me. I have never felt like this before; it is as if I had
dreamed of the sailboat long ago, or had a vision of
it in some other world. For who in this world
would trouble himself so much about a blue sail?

* *Heinrich von Ofterdingen: An Alternative Opening.*

Ian Hamilton Finlay

Cinema-Going

One afternoon in a cinema in the East Neuk when I was about nine years old. The film was *Captains Courageous* with Spencer Tracey and Freddie Bartholemew, the child star. A story of the famous schooners out of Gloucester, Massachusetts, to fish the Grand Banks for cod. Astonishingly, the film projector, concealed in its flimsy little wooden cabin, was powered by the engine of an inshore fishing boat. It *put-putted* all through the 'picture' (as we called a film in those days): *put-put* in the grey fog of the banks, and *put-put* in the half-darkness of the summer afternoon stalls.

Ian Hamilton Finlay

Decommissioned
Recommissioned

for tiller made from salvaged 2 inch planking

FEAR NOT

galvanised mast-fitting, taken from ashes

band of **GOLDEN SHEAF**

for (oak) strongpost, redressed

shorn Samson

for tiller made from pier-pile

know the way home

for bowsprit (spruce thinning)

present another face

for stock of abandoned anchor (iron)

big fisherman, bite into bay

Ian Stephen

For Tan Foresail, in Duradon

                                          to

                           thread

                   you through

            the wind's eye

Ian Stephen

For Black Cotton Cone:
Visual Storm Signal

to

speak

warning

over breaking

and wearing waters

Ian Stephen

A CATALOGUE OF SHIPS

IAN HAMILTON FINLAY
IAN STEPHEN
GRAHAM RICH

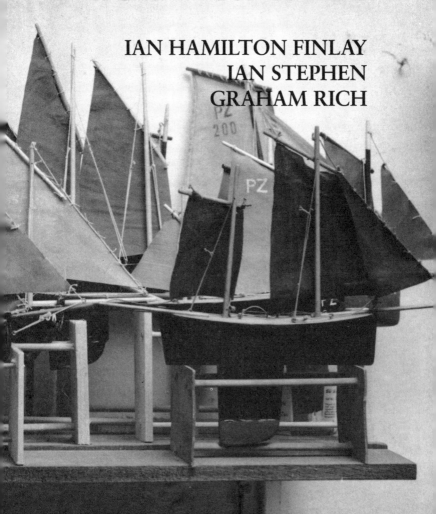

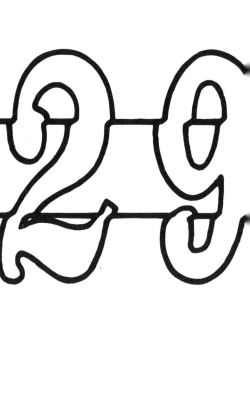

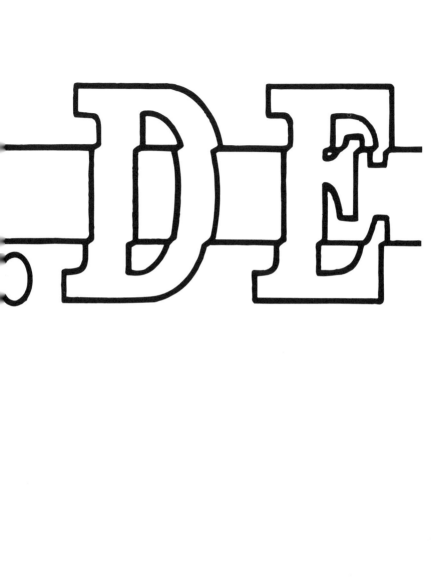

Funnels
Ian Hamilton Finlay with John Andrew
Photograph, David Paterson. 1998.

Ian Stephen. 1998.

Deriva
Graham Rich, Santiago, Chile. 1998.

OPEN SEA

GRAHAM RICH

FEAR NOT

You slept for most of the day. Then woke to inform me you'd had enough of lying around, recovering from *aprés*-ferry syndrome. Now you wanted to do some walking. But I was getting over *aprés*-night-shift syndrome. You gave me that look, through the thick dark fringe. Only if it was all right with me.

I said it would be a bit better than all right and you gave me another look from your repertoire. I was forgetting. Your English was like my sister's bike in the shed. Just needed a skoosh of WD40. A what? Like a lot of things, easier to show than explain.

When it comes to machinery, nothing's impossible. Just that you reach the point of economic viability. We wouldn't get the bike going in the time available. My next shift was looming.

We took the long blue bus out, past the airport. We were the only passengers. The driver admired your hat with the long tassle. Practical kind of thing that, good wind-indicator. You were about to give it away to him and my hand put pressure on your arm. He would have been embarassed.

The sand was invading the tarmac at the turning-place. End of the road. A dry North-easter, not a common wind here. Another man was walking a collie. He recognised me under my new beret. Did I know that an uncle of mine used to come swimming here every day of the year. Running out from near Mossend, so the story went.

The line squalls came at speed over the ebb. Coils from lug-worm casts broke the sandflats between the concrete defences.

From wartime?

No, only the war with the wind and sea.

Now that was real Hebridean Romantic. That will keep your foreign visitor happy.

You've woken up. But you know the best haddock came from there, Broad Bay. And flatfish, usually all just called flounder here but the spotted flounder were plaice. Some the size of skate. You know that fish?

There's a recipe, maybe from North Germany, to cook them with smoked bacon and chopped onion. You make cuts in the skin to take-in all the taste when the ... plaice are cooking. These tenses. I understood her?

The far side of Broad Bay had another recipe for plaice. Like salmon, you don't want to boil them to death. No, of course they were dead but. Anyway, you cleaned the fish and put a good big one in cold water in the biggest pan in the house. Added a bit of salt and pepper and put it on the fire till it came to the boil. Then you took it from the heat. Next you went to the peats or out to take the cow back from the moor. Or coiled some hay or did anything that got you out into the fresh air and made you hungry. Then you came home to eat the fish cold, with your fingers, from its own juice.

And haddock. What was that fish. *Seelax*?

No I don't know the German or the French but I know a book that does. Guy called Alan Davidson. *North Atlantic Seafood*. Bit of a bible. Shit, lent mine to someone. Haddock were about number one here. Still are if you can find one. Nodding out to Broad Bay, out over the blown shallows.

You asked why it was "were", tuned into the language now.

Bigger boats with bigger nets. Just the times. Changes.

But there must be some of the fish left?

The stragglers. It slipped out and I wasn't keen to expand. You pushed me.

From Tolsta to Coll and over the other side of the bay, Portnaguran, Portvoller, wherever they could beach a small boat. They'd go out under oars or a lugsail, with coiled small-lines, ninety or so hooks a line, to take white-fish. Not only in summer. These boats needed a turn of speed. To race out to the grounds and to run from gathering wind. Of course there was rivalry. In Tolsta they favoured the Ness-built boats. In Coll they had some in the Orkney style. A sweeter shape in the stern, some said and that bit extra larch in the sheer behind the helmsman when you were running before a big following sea. You'd place your order to some boatbuilder some side or other of the Pentland Firth. Then go over with your crew to sail her home. Of course all these vessels, Lewis or Orkney, Shetland or Faroes, all have Viking origins. Don't say that too loudly near the boatbuilders though.

And you say you're not religious.

Of course it's religion. Look at the names. *Fear Not. Peace and Plenty.* Passed from vessel to vessel. The 18 ft beach-launched boat. The twenty-five footer to go out the North Minch with the great-lines. The deep-displacement oak on oak hull imported from Denmark in the 60s. Electronics that wouldn't disgrace the Starship Enterprise. And Industrial Fishing. That means you don't eat what you catch. The pout and sandeels scooped from the food-chain and processed to feed chickens or mink or anything else in fur, fins or feathers you can stick in a cage. And I don't care if I am degenerating into high romantic intensity.

So did you fish to make your living?

No you're looking at another student. Sorry. No wild Gaelic fisher. Once though, I made it round Tiumpan Head to fish Broad Bay proper. We'd set out about 5 a.m. from SY. The Sea-Angling Club boat was a 22ft clinker, with a Lister diesel. We'd have been bloody excommunicated if the committee had seen what we had aboard. Not a multiplier reel in sight but baskets and *scumaigs* of coiled lines. We scrounged half a box of herring and I'd to cut twenty slim baits from each one of them. The thing was to keep the hooks in sequence. They'd to pay out, in time, when the heavy sinker plummeted, white bubbles in the green.

Glass day. Only the three of us. And the first line ready to haul when the last was shot. Tiumpan to Tolsta Head. Squiggles of biro on squared paper in the skipper's back pocket, noting positions. The old guys had to grapel to recover their lines sometimes.

Couldn't risk a buoy on the gear in case the trawlermen or drifters went away with the lot. Accidentally-on-purpose.

The first line was over a nursery. A lot of cleaned hooks and here and there a poor immature whiting or haddock. One codling for the basket. A scallop came up holding to a hook. The skipper had it open. Some saint's shellfish, in French. Not Frere Jaques but the man himself. You could eat them like the toffs ate oysters. I watched his throat as he swallowed. It really went down, orange bit and all. I was near sick, seeing another couple on the line. Us two apprentices had to swallow one each. But the salt and sweet taste wasn't so bad. Down it slid.

The second line was heavy. I was near over the side watching for the first fish. But I could feel the line was sluggish, none of the bounce you'd expect from the jumbo haddies.

Spotted dogs. Junior sand-sharks. Over the kennels this time. One on nearly every hook. Hands scraped till you got the knack of holding tail against head so the beast with the beady eyes couldn't take the skin off you.

The third was a string of washing, flapping out in the small current of Broad Bay. Whiting at first but decent ones, not to be sniffed at. Delicate fish. *Merlan.* What's the dish, yes, with slivers of citrus and baked, swallowing their own tails.

A flattie here and there, dabs and small plaice. Then the first of these haddock. The black thumb-mark against a grey side, showing through the water. Then another and another. A torn snood, a bare hook, here and there but the haddies kept coming.

You're out there aren't you? You know the word *angst?*

OK I've been going on. Your innocent enquiry. Regretting it? What's happened to the tranquil Island you're seeking, in retreat from Zurich.

Truth is we were both ready for the return of the bus. We were lucky to catch it at the turning place, the driver lingering to have a smoke.

It was the coldest day of that summer. It made you hungry for hot food. No disrespect to these salads you dressed with mustard and cream. I tried to recreate my mother's broth. Stirred in her high kitchen. We couldn't see the harbour directly but you'd see a high spar crossing a slate roof below you.

I survived the shift as you nearly always do. Hit the bakers on the way home and came in triumphant with brown rolls and the white Scotch loaf with a black crust. You showed me the book over breakfast.

I bought the bible. When you went for your rest. Haddock are *Schellfish*. But they're not St Peter's fish. See, the French, the Norwegians, the Spanish, the Swedish all say John Dory is Peter's fish. The haddock is *Faux St Pierre*.

Well it's a bloody shame the French, Portugese, Spanish, Norwegians, Swedish and every other bastard outside Broad Bay has got it wrong.

But the man in the bookshop said it was the same in Gaelic. *Iasg Pheadair.*

Some pal he turned out.

I wrote it down. This strange fish with spines and a black thumb-print. John Dory. *Haringskonig*, king of the herring, in German and Dutch.

You had the nerve to open the book at the illustrated page. I retreated to the few hours' worth of oblivion I felt entitled to.

You made coffee when I woke. You were ready to see some more of the island. You'd studied the timetables. It was my free night between shifts but I'd a mission this afternoon. The Sea Angling Club would have the weigh-in about five o'clock. I didn't like fishing-competitions but wanted to keep in touch.

The man I'd called the skipper wouldn't be there. He'd gone-off everything to do with clubs and competitions. He'd fallen out with the committee and wasn't too fussed because he'd lost his taste for weighing and photographing big dead fish that didn't always get eaten.

When I went over to the west side of Number One pier, the boats, chartered for the day, were coming in. I had a full oilskin smock on, looking the part, as the rain came down thick. Not much wind behind it. I wore clogs, like the East Coast boys, working on purse-seine nets, taking-up the whole length of Number Two.

I gripped the rope that someone threw. Made the nod. I put weight on that rope but it was against the strain on the gantry. Below me, iron hooks went into the cut-out handles of the bottom fish-box of three, all stacked together. This was one man's catch. He caught my eye. He was one of the Old School.

They'd found a mark, the first for years. I didn't have to ask where they'd come from. A last single fish was placed on the top box. I was about to haul. Paused. Was about to say, wouldn't it be better to take only the one box first.

The block on the gantry was running fine so far. It was working after all. You could see at a glance that these fish had never been in a net. A haul from out the blue. The broad blue.

It became awkward. The three boxes came through an arc and I knew for sure I was pulling from the wrong angle. I wanted to shout again but nothing came out. Wooden boxes glanced against the concrete rim of the pier.

They tumbled back to hit the gunnel just as the swell was taking the boat a yard or so out. The decks were strewn with haddock, a few speckled things amongst them. But most of the grey shapes went to the black harbour water, between the smudged gloss of the boat and the dirty timbers.

If I'd moved quickly, I could have recovered a lot. There had to be a gaff aboard. Below me the guys were just shaking their heads. They knew there wasn't any gaff or long-handled net aboard so there wasn't much point in rushing about. The fat harbour seals would get the fish.

Someone showed me then, how to bring my end of the rope round to the other side of that post, so the angle was correct. Hooks went into handles again and this time boxes came up, smoothly enough, one by one, to outstretched arms.

That's the full story of the *schellfish*, the story I failed to tell you when you returned hungry, from your big walk. I just pointed to the bundle of newspapers by the sink. We unwrapped them together and, even faded, they were still beauties. We were hearing one another breathing. You said it —
These are the real St Peter's fish.
I took the knife to one and you shuddered. Its head was left on and I took its white liver to mix with oatmeal, seasoning and a touch of chopped onion. The stuffing went back through the mouth, down to the gills. You were horrified. This is the only way. Just simmered, whole like a salmon, but in milk, with leeks. A forkful of butter. A turn of black pepper, falling to the white and green and grey.
Tell it to stop looking at me.
You were sad at the head with eyes gone opaque in their sockets. At me seeking the white meat from its cheeks. But you tasted it all. Then came back to it again, even the *cean cropaig*. Not just so you could say you'd tasted our traditions. That's why I'm thinking of you now and why I want to get close to you by not keeping things back from you.
I couldn't say it then as I couldn't admit to my part in the waste of fish, the spilled boxes. Maybe if I'd been able to talk and then just listen, after the lyrical bits, we might have touched. If we'd touched and held together you might have come back to me.

Ian Stephen

STROMNESS, FROM THE HARBOUR

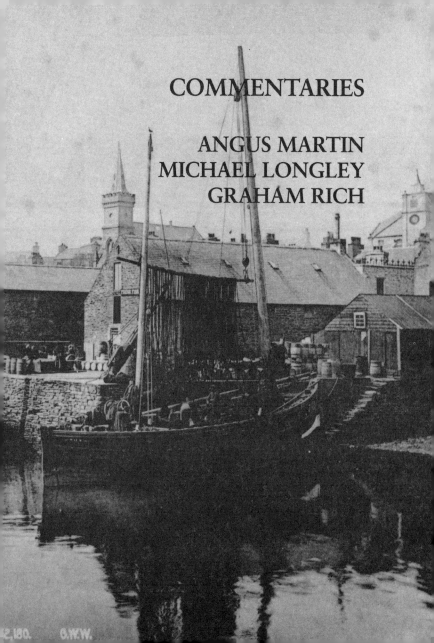

COMMENTARIES

ANGUS MARTIN
MICHAEL LONGLEY
GRAHAM RICH

RING-NETTERS

If the truth be told, I was never much of a fisherman. Five years are sufficient to obtain a master's degree at an institute of learning, but the same period of time proved insufficient to make a complete fisherman of me. None the less, what I did learn has since informed every branch of my writing and imbued me with an enduring love of the lore of fishing and of the boats themselves.

Not the generality of boats that I see nowadays – lumpish, bristly things – but those boats whose lives I shared and whose beauty of form is, for me, encapsulated in this memory. Leaving Carradale harbour on a summer evening in 1973 and heading south into a heavy bound, I was lying on the foredeck and watching the *Harvest Queen* off to port on a parallel course, lifting so that her lower hull was bared before she fell over and lifted again, her slender curves fleetingly exposed. I was glimpsing then the timeless grace of a boat in rhythmic motion, and I have never forgotten it.

I was also seeing an evolutionary form in its final manifestation – the post-war ring-netter, descended from the fully-decked prototypes of 1922, the *Falcon* and the *Frigate Bird,* which supplanted the part-decked Loch Fyne Skiffs, these, in 1882, with the *Alpha* and the *Beta,* themselves marking the demise of the small open skiffs with which ring-netting began in the 1830s.

What they all had in common, these apparently disparate boat-types, was a suitability for certain operational conditions. The ring-net fishing grounds were predominantly the narrow sea-lochs and kyles of the Clyde and West Coast, and the boats pursued herring right to the shore-head. In order to 'ring' herring speedily in these confined and often congested seaways, the boats were required to 'turn on a sixpence', as the old men would say.

I was privileged to play a part in the preservation, in 1995, of one of the best-known of the post-war ringers, the *Watchful*. A 56-footer, she was built in 1959 by Weatherhead and Blaikie of Port Seton for the Sloan brothers, Matt and Billy, of Maidens.

As the *Stella Maris* of Campbeltown, she had been decommissioned and was due to be broken up; but, with the aid of the late Andy Alexander – who had fished with the *Watchful* from her arrival in Maidens until her departure in 1972 – the boat was secured by the then Kyle and Carrick District Council, to become a terrestrial display-piece at Ayr harbour.

The Sloans were ring-net fishermen *par excellence*. Among the fishing communities of the West coast their prowess became legendary. Matt, now 81, skippered the *Watchful*, while Billy had the neighbour-boat, the *Wistaria,* for ring-netting was a two-boat operation. I use the past tense, because the method had died out, and with it a range of skills and a distinctive lifestyle.

From Girvan, Maidens and Dunure, fleets of graceful motor ringers fished the Clyde and the farther grounds of the Minches, Isle of Man, Firth of Forth and Yorkshire coast. Such families as the Sloans, Gemmells, McCrindles and McCreaths became synonymous with success.

Skilled ring-net men there certainly were elsewhere – in Campbeltown, Carradale, Tarbert and beyond – but the best of the Ayrshiremen had, for me at least, a magic, a mystique that set them above the others. Was it greater commitment, superior skill, or – that much-debated indefinable, never far from the fisherman's superstitious view of the world – better 'luck'? I don't pretend to know.

Even their boats' names had, to an exceptional degree, that same magical quality: *New Dawn, Fair Morn, Fair Wind, Storm Drift, Arctic Moon, Pathfinder, Valhalla, Saffron, Sapphire, Taeping, Jasmine, Huntress.*

Ring-netters were beautiful boats that anyone might admire, and they were maintained like yachts. The job itself, of course, was kind to the boats, which – to use an equine analogy – were thoroughbreds compared with the ungainly workhorses that now predominate.

In springtime, when herring fishing was slack, they would be beached and cleaned. Everything moveable was taken ashore, and the boats made spotless inside and out. Hulls would be sanded back to the bare wood and given up to five coats of varnish (the paint-pot was resorted to only when the wood had begun to blacken with age.) At least six weeks would be spent 'on the beach', and the remarkable thing is that the work was essentially unpaid. But the men had pride in the boats and wanted them to look their best. And they did.

Angus Martin

PAPER BOATS

Catalogues which release the power of names by stringing them together to make rhythmic sense are at the heart of poetry and go all the way back to the catalogue of ships in Homer's *Iliad*. There are so many catalogues in my own work, I sometimes feel I should ration them. But they continue to happen, especially at heightened moments, and I prefer to drift with what seems a natural tendency. Ian Hamilton Finlay's example makes me feel that I am right to do so. Each time a catalogue creeps into a poem I am reminded of his beautiful 'Green Waters' which consists solely of the names of trawlers. Since I first discovered it in the Sixties, this poem has had a huge influence on me. I return to its twelve short lines again and again. I have not visited Homer's catalogue of ships nearly as often! 'Green Waters' taught me to scribble down lists of things before I could be sure of their relevance. Each of the four quatrains of my poem 'Trade Winds' consists of a short catalogue: the names of the locks on the River Lagan, of the apples from County Armagh, of clay pipes manufactured in Carrickfergus, and of fishing smacks in Portavogie harbour. The last of these allowed me to say as much about life and death in twenty-four words as I am ever likely to manage in so confined a space. The skippers who had so suggestively christened their boats offered me the poem, as it were, and Ian Hamilton Finlay showed me how to accept it:

> Among the Portavogie prawn-fishermen
> Which will be the ship of death: Trade Winds,
> Guiding Starlight, Halcyon, Easter Morn,
> Liberty, Faithful Promise, Sparkling Wave?

Some years ago when I was away from home looking for wild flowers in the Burren in County Clare, the man who worked in our local ice cream shop in Belfast was murdered by paramilitaries. When I tried to write an elegy for him, I opened the little green notebook into which I had jotted down flower names. I worked hard to turn them into a wreath of words, a prayer of sorts, and ended the elegy with a catalogue of the wild flowers I had seen in the Burren in one day. Later, the ice cream man's mother wrote to thank me for the poem: "The fact that there were twenty-one flavours of ice cream, and you wrote twenty-one flowers was coincidental," she told me. But it was more than a coincidence. My elegy and her heartbreaking letter would not exist if I had not summoned up 'Green Waters', felt reverence for the flower names and taken time to write them down.

Flower names. Boat names. When recently I discovered Finlay's 'Ovidian Flowers', I was overwhelmed by a feeling of kinship, which was further intensified by our shared fixations on Ovid and the world wars. Even without its gloss his poem is ravishing:

> *Veronica* became *Temptress*
> *Hibiscus* became *Spry*
> *Arabis* became *Saucy*
> *Periwinkle* became *Restless*
> *Calendula* became *Ready*
> *Begonia* became *Impulse*
> *Larkspur* became *Fury*
> *Heartsease* became *Courage*
> *Candytuft* became *Tenacity*

But the gloss takes us so much further and generates truly Ovidian transformations: "Early in 1942 U-boat successes against American merchant shipping resulted in a number of Flower Class corvettes being transferred from the RN to the

USN." The poem and its gloss are printed on either side of a card that is smaller than a postcard. At first this seems an eccentric way to publish such remarkable work. But 'Ovidian Flowers' and all the other poem-cards and leaflets and posters modify our notions of how an oeuvre might accumulate. They also suggest that *sub specie aeternitatis* only a handful of poems will make it; that this could be one of them; that in any case every poem is a memorandum to posterity.

As though in recognition of the fact that our civilisation is paper-thin, Finlay throughout his career has remained loyal to paper, the flimsiest of materials. But he has also worked in wood and stone. Whatever the medium, he writes words down and gives them their place. Like Saint Colmcille he has left his fingerprints in stone. The virtuoso of the confined space, he turns on a sixpence:

Dove, dead in its snows

What more needs to be said? Finlay captures the moment of inspiration, and in a split second transports us from inkling to transfiguration. With its roots in the Latin *movere,* to move, 'momentous' which relates to 'moment' (a point of time, an instant) and means important, weighty, is the adjective I'm tempted to choose for Finlay's work. But 'momentous' doesn't really do justice to his quick-silver imagination, or the way he combines the witty with the devout. Such word-play and suggestiveness of image resist tidy epithets. It is easier for me to imagine Ian Hamilton Finlay folding paper boats for the boy Odysseus and launching them, happy-go-lucky, in the direction of Troy.

Michael Longley

VANITY

I can remember the day my life changed. I had a little seven foot rowing boat and I used to spend all my summer holidays trying to keep the water out of it. I used to put Seelastic into it and bitumen and tar. All that used to happen was that the tar and bitumen used to wash right out. So it was a continuous job, keeping her caulked. I had these big fisherman's waders I used to get out to the boat. So my world of boating was muddy and tarry and wet.

I dared to go into Topsham Sailing Club. I wasn't a member. I was a little in awe of it. And there before me was the most beautiful thing I had seen in my ten years of life. It was a Hornet class dinghy with a mark 5 deck-plan. And it had rolled Sapele decks and it had a high-cambered foredeck which made the whole thing look a little bit like a torpedo. It was gleaming in the sun and it had a rich grain, a lovely intensity. These rolled decks were doubling up as buoyancy tanks and I could not believe how they could be watertight, having striven so hard to make *my* boat watertight. The owner came out of the sailing club. He took one look at me and said, don't get mud on that.

I had been transported into a new world of things. I had not known that such beautiful objects existed and that people were capable of making such things, in wood. And that people were capable of sailing them and of possessing them. The mark 5 Hornet was beautiful but the 505 was better. And the Merlin Rocket was even more sumptuous. Even more perfect. We used to go, as schoolboys, down to Rowsell's boatbuilding yard to look at perfection, just to gasp at it and touch it. Every little detail, every little vanity was unbelievable. Each little fitting, each little control-line cleat, each little cam-cleat, each little spinnaker cleat would have its own little plinth, its own little sculptured turret, the function of which was just to lift the fitting enough to get a 4 millimetre rope under it. Just to facilitate

84

cleating and uncleating, the fitting would have this little mount but each mount was individually sculpted to fit the characteristics of the fitting. And the plinth would be glued and sanded. It would be made of mahogany. The mahogany would have a horizontal thread of white sycamore through it, just a little laminate that was barely perceptible, as thin as your fingernail. Sometimes these lines would fade in the sun. Sometimes they would fade-out. They were that delicate. Finding them was always very thrilling. The carlin – that's the inner edge of the deck of the Merlin Rocket – always had two little threads of sycamore running through it. Sycamore was very difficult to find. There was only one week in the year they reckoned you could cut sycamore. And if you cut it before or after that week it would get black in it from the sap. The sap wouldn't get fully dried-out. I remember doing a deck-job on a Lark dinghy and trying to get sycamore. And it was like, "I don't know, I don't know, I know where you might get sycamore." But it was only stuff that someone else had rejected because of this black sap in it which we had to try to cut out.

Epoxy resin has made wood more permanent and more practical. But the fashion now for racing dinghies is to have everything white. The all-white, glass-fibre, one-design, off-the-shelf, out-of-the-box boat. That sumptuousness – a lot of that has been lost. Much of it was vanity. It wasn't functional, it wasn't necessary. I remember an editor of the American *Wooden Boat* magazine, he called in at Rowsell's boatyard and he bought a Merlin Rocket. He didn't buy it to sail it. He bought it to possess it. These things have a life. They're not beautiful for ever. They get shabby and they get knocked-about and in the end they die. In those dinghy parks. Stinging nettles grow over them. They have a history. They do become obsolete. The designs become superseded by faster designs. So they've this fantastic burn, this turnover – as part of the culture of racing.

There's a Scottish myth, I've been told about, that Scottish workboats are very functional in the way they're decorated. They're not over-embellished. They're not objects of vanity. They're objects of utility and the myth is that the sea can become envious of boats which are too beautiful. The sea will want to possess the boat for herself. So there's a caution here that we should not indulge ourselves, should not indulge our necessity for beauty too much or the sea will come and steal it away.

Graham Rich

NOTES

Port Registrations: SY – Stornoway; HH – Hamburg; E – Exeter; LO – London. Postcodes: EH – Edinburgh; Imagined Lands: LS – Little Sparta.

All commercial fishing vessels are registered with a major port. Some also boats bear the name of their home port or village painted on the stern.

Wooden boats of traditional construction can be divided into two types: *clinker*, overlapping planks, and *carvel*, flush planks. A *Zulu* is a type of lugger; it has a steeply raked stern, while a *Fifie's* sternpost is almost vertical, in relation to the keel.

Broad Bay: an 18 foot Stroma yole (larch on oak) built in Durness in 1912 and used for inshore line fishing on Lewis, most of its working life. First registered in Kirkwall, then Stornoway, SY 574. A yawl, a *yole* shaped boat, double ended, with hollow garboards, more or less deadrise, flared flanks and raked ends. *Broad Bay* is now owned by Ian Stephen and rigged with a stand–ing-lug (made in Duradon, by James Lawrence of Brightlingsea).

SY 273 Fear Not: Danish-built (oak on oak) Motor Fishing Vessel. Engaged in industrial fishing and trawling in the North Minch and Broad Bay. Decommissioned six years ago following a fire on board and broken up in 1996. This name has been given to generations of vessels, mainly of *Sgoth Niseach* type, working from Tolsta, Isle of Lewis.

Emily: 15 foot Westray skiff, built in Orkney circa 1912 and imported to Lewis. The vessel lay derelict on the shoreline of Stornoway harbour since 1995, and was broken up by gales in March 1997. Parts of *Emily* returned to Orkney for the *Green Waters* exhibition.

Jouissance: 24 foot Mark 1 Cornish Crabber, built at Rock, Cornwall in 1978. Now owned by Graham Rich and Lesley Kerman, she is a topsail Gaff Cutter. Her design is closely related to the West Country working boats of the late 19th century.

Portrona: the old name for the port of Stornoway.
The Chicken: rock landmark off Swordale, Lewis.
Brightlingsea: in Essex, one of the cinque ports.
Pittenweem: fishing port in the Kingdom of Fife.

Prologue

'Always Boats and Men': from Angus Martin's second collection,*The Song of the Quern* (Scottish Cultural Press, 1998). Martin is also the author of *The Ring-Net Fishermen,* a classic history of the Scottish ring-net fishing industry (John Donald, 1981). He was born into a fishing family in 1952, in Campbeltown, and still lives and work there.

'Zulu Fishing': Norman Malcolm MacDonald is a dramatist, novelist and poet. He lives in Tong, Isle of Lewis. 'Zulu Fishing' is from *Portrona*, a play describing the lives of the fishing community in the 1890s, first performed in the transit shed, Number One Pier, Stornoway, 1996.

'Seeker Reaper': first published in *Wind on Loch Fyne* (Oliver & Boyd, 1948). It describes the lives of the fishermen in Campbell Hay's native Loch Fyne. His *Collected Poems* will appear from Polygon in the Autumn of 1998. Glossary: *solan* – solan goose, gannet; *stieve* – stiff; *peerie* – wee, small (like a spinning top); *coulter* – cutting blade at the fore end of a ploughshare.

'Joy in the Hebrides': Kevin MacNeil was born in Stornoway; he writes in Gaelic and English. His first collection, *Love and Zen in the Outer Hebrides* (Canongate, 1998) features a photo by Ian Stephen on its cover. Glossary: *mi-chailear* – unpleasant, gloomy; *geansaidh* – gansey, jersey.

'Fisherfolk at Newhaven': from 'Settlements', a long poem exploring place and memory. David Octavius Hill and Robert Adamson were pioneers of photography. *The Fishermen and Women of the Firth of Forth,* their photographic record of the Newhaven fishing community was published by the Scottish National Galleries in 1991. John Burnside lives in Cellardyke, a short walk from the Scottish Fisheries Museum.

Green Waters

'Green Waters': composed from the names of British fishing boats.

'Providence': from a sequence of love poems to the author's wife, Barbara Ziehm, first published in *Varying States of Grace* (Polygon, 1989). The 'Arnish light' and 'the Beacon' are navigational aids for entering Stornoway harbour.

'Vernacular Shaping of a Sailing Vessel': Topher Dawson's boat-building yard is in Scoraig, Wester Ross. He collaborated with Stephen on a permanent boat-based sculpture for An Tobar, Isle of Mull.

'Five Poems for Nine Planks': realised by Stephen for the exhibition *Green Waters*; planks, or *strakes*, were made from Scots-grown larch and cut at Topher Dawson's yard to follow the lines of a Westray skiff, as supplied by Ian Richardson, boat–builder, Stromness.

'River Exe': navigates the short voyage down the River Exe from Graham Rich's home at Topsham to Turf Lock.

'creels and creels': the original version by the Swiss Concrete poet Eugen Gomringer is here transformed by Finlay into pastoral by exchanging the nouns – 'net ropes' for elevators' etc – for those in the Loeb translation of Theocritus' *Idylls*.

'The Inscriptions': Gilonis' poem is a homage to the American poet Carl Rakosi: see J. D. Beazley, *Attic Red-Figure Vase-Painters*, (Clarendon

Press, 1963, Appendix IV). Finlay's response was first published in his *Echoes Series* (1995); see F. S. Cooper, *A Handbook of Sailing Barges*, (Adlard Coles Ltd., 1955).

'Expectation': the original is by the German Romantic author Novalis (pen name of Friedrich Leopold Von Hardenberg); his 'blue flowers', a symbol of romantic yearning, are here replaced with a blue sail.

A Catalogue of Ships

'A boatshelf': the minature boat models – mostly *Fifies* and *Zulus* – are by Ian Hamilton Finlay. The photograph is by Robin Gillanders.

'529.DE': Ian Hamilton Finlay with Gary Hincks; titled *Clinker Built*, first published in 1997.

'gooseneck' and 'yard': poems on the spars of *Broad Bay*, the former made by John Murdo MacLeod and the latter from a derelict *sgoth*, after serving many years as a clothes pole.

'Idyll': an idyll on Lochan Eck, Little Sparta; the photograph is by Pia Simig (1998).

'Deriva': match box boats made by Graham Rich, sailing in a drainage channel in Santiago, Chile. *Deriva* – to drift or to be adrift. *I noticed that each morning water spilled into the culvert, but by late afternoon it had dried again. I set myelf a three-day task to see how eight match box boats would become relocated with each daily tidal flood.*

Open Sea

'Approaching Brixham': *Jouissance* approaching the Victoria Break–water at Brixham (Devon). The wood is a fragment of David McCabe's boat *Patience*.

'Surviving the Lizard' (the cover is a detail from this work): *This was made in anticipation rounding the Lizard on a return voyage from the Scillies. When we actually arrived at the Lizard there was thick fog. On my return home I painted fog onto the work, obscuring the word Lizard which had previously been painted onto the wood.*

'The Loom of the Lighthouse': made from wood found in Blagdon's Boatyard, Plymouth.

'Open Sea: Cornwall': one of a series of tryptichs made in 1998.

'Day Six': from *Eighteen Day voyage – Chile,* made from an offcut of a larger work.

'Rounding Dodman Point': *a notorious Cornish headland where we learnt to respect tidal streams.*

'Day Twelve': *My Daughter Ellie found this piece in a land fill site by the side of the road. I painted it green with table tennis paint.*

'Day Four – Red Door' (detail): *A refuse truck was coming down the road at El Tabo – a man ran out of his house with this piece of wood and leant it against his dust bin. I crossed the road and picked it up.*

Fear Not

Glossary: *Coupes St Jacques* – scallop; *John Dory* or *Zeus Faber,* called *Iasg Phadair* in Gaelic and Peter's fish in most Northern European languages; *flattie* – collective for inshore flatfish: dab, flounder, plaice, lemon-sole.

Commentaries

The photograph of Stromness harbour circa 1890 is by George Washington Wilson. The Pier Arts Centre is just visible on the quay to the right.

Michael Longley, born in Belfast, 1939; his most recent collection is *The Ghost Orchid* (Jonathan Cape, 1995).

'Vanity': from a recording of Graham Rich's conversation aboard *Broad Bay,* Lochmaddy Boat Festival, June 1998.

AUTHOR NOTES

Graham Rich

Born 1945, Devon.

Lives in Topsham, where the River Exe flows past the foot of his garden. Studied at Exeter College of Art and Bristol University, gained a Masters at Exeter University. Taught Art at Exeter College for many years. From the age of ten his diaries contain details of boatbuilding, boat tuning, dinghy races and voyages around the coast to Cornwall. Since 1985 these voyages have become the subject of his art, providing the experiences, and the materials from which his art is made.

Publications: *Open Sea*, Moschatel Press (1990).

Exhibitions: Exe Gallery, Exeter (1983); Cairn Gallery, Nailsworth (1988, 1990, 1991, 1997, 1998), East West Gallery, London (1991); Gordon Hepworth Gallery (1992, 1994, 1995, 1996, 1997); Swansea Arts Workshop Gallery (1993, 1997); Dillington House, Somerset (1995); Victoria Gallery, Bath, (1998).

Ian Hamilton Finlay

Born Nassau, Bahamas, 1925.

Ian Hamilton Finlay is internationally recognised as a poet and as Scotland's foremost living artist. The sea has always been a strong theme running through his work, from the poems he wrote in the 1950s on Rousay, Orkney, to his Concrete poems of the 1960s, and in the inland garden he created with Sue Finlay at *Little Sparta*. Over the past four decades Finlay has published hundreds of books, booklets, poem prints, folding cards and postcards celebrating boats and the sea. A Catalogue Raisonné of his prints was published by Cantz in 1997.

Ian Stephen

Born Stornoway, Isle of Lewis, 1955.

Graduated from Aberdeen University. Worked for many years as a Coastguard Officer on the Isle of Lewis. Now runs Last House Writing Centre and Studio, on Lewis. Much of his work centred on repairing, sailing and fishing from his boat *Broad Bay*.

Publications include: *Malin, Hebrides, Minches* (Dangaroo Press, 1983), *Varying States of Grace* (Polygon, 1989), *Suid an t-Eilean* (Editor, Acair, 1993), *Buoyage* (with Will Maclean, Morning Star Publications, 1993), *A Semblance of Steerage* (Morning Star Publications, 1994), *Broad Bay* (Morning Star Publications/An Lanntair/City Art Centre, 1997), *Time & Tide* (with David Connearn, Morning Star Publications, 1998).

Many recent exhibitions, performances, and workshops, often in collaboration with artists.

Published in an edition of 1500 copies
on the occasion of the exhibition *Green Waters*

The Pier Arts Centre, Stromness
29 August – 26 September, 1998

Peacock Printmakers, Aberdeen
16 January – 27 February, 1999

Taigh Chearsabhagh, Lochmaddy
North Uist
29 April – 28 May, 1999

Acknowledgments

© Ian Hamilton Finlay: *Proem*, IHF/Ron Costley, (1997); *Green Waters, Poor.Old.Tired.Horse.*, (No. 15, 1966); *The English Colonel*, from *Orkney Lyrics* in *The Dancers Inherit the Party* (Migrant Press, 1960, reprinted in an expanded edition Polygon, 1996), *Proverbs* (1997); *The Inscriptions (for Harry Gilonis)*, from *Echoes Series*, (1995); *Cinema Going*, (1998, previously unpublished); *Boatshelf*, IHF/Dave Paterson, (1998); *Idyll*, IHF/Pia Simig, (1998)

Unless stated otherwise these were first published by Wild Hawthorn Press. Details of publications for sale are available from Stonypath, Little Sparta, Dunsyre, Lanark.

© Ian Stephen: *Fear Not* photograph, first published in *Providence II*, The Windfall Press, (1993); *Providence*, from *Varying States of Grace,* © Polygon (1989)

Photographs of *KY136 Hope* and *KY64* © Diane Tammes, first published in *The Olsen Excerpts*, © Ian Hamilton Finlay (Verlag Udo Breger, 1971); Photograph of Stromness harbour, George Washington Wilson, courtesy of Stromness Museum; *Seeker Reaper*, George Campbell Hay, © W. L. Lorimer Trust; *Joy in the Hebrides*, © Kevin MacNeil, *Love and Zen in the Outer Hebrides*, © Canongate Books (1998); *Fisherfolk Newhaven*, © John Burnside; *Zulu Fishing*, © Norman Malcolm MacDonald; *Always Boats and Men*, © Angus Martin, from *The Song of the Quern*, © Scottish Cultural Press (1998), *Ring-Netters*, © Angus Martin; *The Inscriptions (for Carl Rakosi)*, © Harry Gilonis 1995; *Paper Boats*, © Michael Longley (previously unpublished).

With thanks to
Pia Simig, Barbara Ziehm, Zoë Irvine, Lesley Kerman, Harry Gilonis, Topher Dawson, Angus Martin, Aline Heudeline, Tom Clark, Michael Tucker, Space Explorations, La Mancha International School of Image and Gesture, Chile, Stromness Museum, and especial thanks to Cluny Sheeler for editorial assistance in the making of this book.